Advance Praise
for Hummingwords
and
The Luminous In-Between

As a participant in Cynthia Leslie-Bole's *Hummingwords* writing group, it continually astounds me how such multi-layered images appear to spill out of her so effortlessly. Her writing is at once accessible and profound. I am always left wanting to hear more.
Adina Sara
Author, *Blind Shady Bend*

Cynthia Leslie-Bole's gift is luminosity. Her words elate and inspire her audience.
Donna Kaulkin
Author, *Brenda Corrigan Went Downtown*

I know Cynthia Leslie-Bole as a fellow writer in a women's writing group, where she was a shining star. Her command of the English language inspired everyone in our group. Read her brilliant poetry and you too will be inspired.
Marianne Gage
Author, *The Wind Came Running, The Putneyville Fables*

Cynthia Leslie-Bole is the real deal—not only as a channel for her own accrued wisdom and sensitive observations of the world, but also apparently as a direct channel for higher power and spirit. She interweaves this with a mastery of the craft of writing in a way that deeply nourishes me as both a teacher and a writer.
Melanie Light
Author, *Valley of Shadows and Dreams* and *Coal Hollow*,
Founding Executive Director, *Fotovision*

In this collection Cynthia Leslie-Bole courageously, but with tender fingers, unsheathes the experiences of childhood, marriage, and motherhood and questions what it means to be who she is, now that children have fledged. Through her poetry, she recognizes her own essence as her lifelong companion, and she realizes that although she has changed over the years, that essential spirit will abide with her as she listens for its voice and follows its wisdom "into the waiting arms of her future self". These are poems of rare honesty and insight into the luminous spaces between our first breath and our last. For me as a reader, Cynthia's poems shine light on the subtleties of the choices

I am making in my life and allow me to see the world in a new way through her insightful lens. Cynthia is my personal statue of liberty who indeed lifts her "lamp beside the golden door," illuminating the space between past and future—the present moment.

Sally Bolger
Author, *Greenhorn goes to ANWR blog*

Cynthia Leslie-Bole is a facilitator of writing groups and coach to other writers, and she is stellar in these roles. But beneath the mentor lies a gifted writer, one who not only communicates ideas, but vividly expresses her mind, heart and soul. Cynthia creates paintings of words, filling up her poetic canvas with colors and nuances that sometimes startle and always invite the reader into a shared experience. She layers her writing with language that opens up the imagination, stimulates the vision of the reader, and always touches the heart.

C'Anna Bergman-Hill
Author, *Journeys* and *Dear Mrs. B: The Unplanned Lessons of a Special Education Teacher*

Cynthia Leslie-Bole is one of the wisest, bravest, and most visionary of teachers and coaches. She is a wing-builder who sees the potential in even the smallest seed and knows how to nurture, protect and give it flight. Most of us have endured a lifetime of creative injury, a mountain of judgment and negativity that blocks us from expressing our truth. Cynthia knows how to disassemble that mountain and how to replace it with encouragement and love. Cynthia is a midwife for the manifestation of the soul on paper . . . and in life.

When I first came to Cynthia, I was holding the beaten body of a dying dream. Cynthia believed in my dream and in the strength of her belief, I found hope, light, and a way forward. She has the same transformative effect on all who write with her, encouraging and supporting the words that would otherwise have been lost forever. The depth of her compassion and wisdom is further reflected in her writing. The fruit of all her service to others is a profound insight into life and love—which then becomes her poetry. In fact, Cynthia's *life* is her poetry, and it pours with equal eloquence onto the page.

Elizabeth Perlman
Founder and CEO of *The Intuitive Writing Project*

Cynthia Leslie-Bole's poetry revels in the treasure that language is for her. A reader plunges in, scooping up handfuls of jewels and coins and mysterious tokens of other worlds as they tumble and click and catch the light—providing pleasures for all the senses.

Laura Wine Paster
Poet and *Amherst Writers and Artists Method* leader

When I read Cynthia Leslie-Bole's poetry, I transform from human being to a feathered friend, from mundane subsistence to magical flight or from a broken body to a mended soul. Cynthia is a vessel for words that cascade onto the page with grace and magnitude. Reading her poems is like going on retreat for me.

Mary Tuchscherer
Founder and CEO, *Voiceflame International*

Cynthia Leslie-Bole's poetry reflects life as she does: purely, magically, lovingly, without judgment or a personal agenda. She's a keen observer of reality with an uncanny ability to describe what she sees in multitudes of ways, capturing many different possibilities within any single moment. She's like a prism that takes in a beam of light and refracts a rainbow of color that ordinarily can't be seen with the human eye.

Maureen Brown
CFO of *The Intuitive Writing Project*

I have been blessed to be part of the *Hummingwords* writing workshop facilitated by Cynthia Leslie-Bole. Over the years, I have heard Cynthia read her poetry, prose and stories in the "raw", and they have taken my breath away. I have also had the privilege of reading her edited work. Painstakingly polished images have struck my heart with their beauty and their honesty. Both personal and universal, her poetry explores what it is to be part earth and part spirit as a wife, mother, daughter, and woman. Her love of words is apparent in every line, and her imagery is visceral, touchable, and vibrantly colored. It is grounded in earth and carried by water and wind. Cynthia mines the depths of what it is to be human, to be here. One can only say, yes, yes, that's it.

Cynthia Hoffman
***Hummingwords* writer**

It is difficult to believe that Cynthia Leslie-Bole's distinctive talent has remained under the national radar for so long. Her exuberant and transcendent voice, her wisdom and her emotional power are inspirational. She has a unique and magical way with words. This book is a gift to every poetry lover on the planet.

Shari Nagy
Hummingwords writer

Cynthia Leslie-Bole's poetry is steeped in her grasp of the natural world and woven with open heart and eyes, and the depth of her language makes it a rich read. It follows both journey and random observation. It's honest and brave, and it illuminates feelings, reflections, growth and life. In addition, the forms her words take on the page are visually gorgeous. The form is soft, interesting and unique without ever being distracting or contrived. Brilliant.

Mari Tischenko
Hummingwords writer

The Luminous In Between

poems

Cynthia Leslie-Bole

Azalea Art Press
Southern Pines, North Carolina

ISBN: 978-1-943471-09-6

Cover Painting
by Cynthia Leslie-Bole

For

Ben, Haley, and Holden Leslie-Bole:
my home.

and

Mimi and Don Leslie:
my foundation.

Contents

Marrow

Earth

Foreword

When I followed a whim and signed up for an *Amherst Writers and Artists* (AWA) workshop a decade ago, something akin to a personal miracle happened. After twenty-five years of using literary, technical, and marketing writing as a means to achieving academic and professional advancement, I rediscovered creative writing, something I had loved as a child but forgotten in my push to enter the adult world.

Once the gates were open, torrents of expression gushed forth in all genres as I wrote in my weekly writing groups. For ten years now, I have ventured with my fellow writers over and over into uncharted creative terrain, making discoveries and sharing surprises as we go. It has been a joyful, inspiring journey, and I have often been astonished at the words that have ended up on my pages.

The poems in this collection represent my attempts to understand deeper truths than I am able to perceive when distracted by the bustle of daily life. With its distilled, condensed language, poetry helps me awaken to greater awareness, clarify what's most important, and crystalize moments of wisdom and healing. The subject matter varies, but all of my poems are profoundly personal reflections of my struggles and insights, as well as my awe and wonder at the world around me.

Pat Schneider, founder of the AWA method, and author of *How the Light Gets In: Writing as a Spiritual Practice,* puts it succinctly:

> Writing . . . is where we humans most make our own minds visible to ourselves and others. There, on the faint lines of our pages, we can take down our masks…. In writing, we see, sometimes with fear and trembling, who we have been, who we really are, and . . . who we might become. (p. 99)

Over the years, poetry has allowed me to explore and express my idiosyncratic understanding of who I have been, who I am presently, and who I hope to someday become. The poems in this book are the fruits of that ongoing creative adventure.

Before You Disappear

write before you disappear

write to give shape to your shifting form
to hang muscle and flesh
on the bones of your story
to solidify your shimmering soul

write to feel your way through the dark
to let your thoughts flow ahead like light
and stream behind in a phosphorescent wake

write to create a map
through the dragon territories you've explored
to hold up your words like gemstones
proving treasure awaits others too

write to investigate mirage and shadow
to pursue intimations of meaning
to unearth the truth
from where it lies entombed

write to own instead of borrow
to know instead of suspect
to discover what's right for you
just for you

write to grapple your questions to the ground
pin them in the mud
and stare into their coy eyes
until an answer, any answer
takes shape in the muck

write to express
matter disintegrating into energy
so that even disappearing
has a voice

write to become visible
to your
self

The Luminous In Between

Mirrors

To Imagine My Essence

I reverently peel off
locks of hair
layers of skin
ropes of muscle
and drape them on
my dressmaker's dummy
to preserve their form

I cradle organs
like infants
placing them
in a mossy vivarium
to preserve their
moist plumpness
handling with
exquisite tenderness
eyes, heart, and womb

I take apart my skeleton
bone by bone
and lay the pieces out
one by one
on papyrus inscribed
with inky outlines
like a peg board
bearing ghosts
of absent tools

I use special care
with tiny ear bones
foot bones
hand bones
so as not to lose a piece
vital to listening or walking
writing or waving

I collect blood and lymph
and other liquids of life
in filigreed chalices
inset with rubies
then set them on an altar
in places of
highest honor

and then
finally
there I am

naked essence

a golden sun
shot through with
cobalt and lapis lights
containing the scope
of ocean and sky
and extending out
and out
and out
with fingers of flame
that lick the edges
of the infinite
creative fire

I imagine my essence
stripped down
glowing
gloriously exposed
and after basking
in its fullness
living in its wholeness
letting its light
sear my consciousness
and transmute all sense of self

I reassemble
the beautiful bits
of this sacred vessel
that contains
my own
small
precious portion
of
all that is

the portal is
the moment
where mind opens
and what's real rushes in

the nubbly sidewalk
the tarry parking lot
the cars blithely
maneuvering into slots
then suddenly
the bird
the crow
the huddled bundle of feathers
parked in a too-huge space
delineated by very straight
white lines
life flickering on and off
in a body remembering flight
in a voice echoing
lost morning warbles
the stalled crow
blue-black sheen
dulled with dust
toes curling around asphalt
instead of branch

the homeless man
the busy woman
gather to witness
the body heaving
the beak opening
the tongue darting
the lids drawing
opaque curtains across
obsidian eyes
as cars cruise by
with AC on high

time collapses
to one still point
the black hole of crow
in holy retreat
of spirit from flesh

I am the woman
watching
with impotent compassion
I am the vagrant
shrugging
with philosophical detachment
I am the bird
feeling life wane
choosing not to struggle
letting what's next begin
I am the white lines
containing it all

I am
breath
no breath
and
the luminous
in-between

Creature Comfort

can I say
I love this
white haired creature?

after 54 and 3/4 springs
have baked into summer
and flamed into fall
after 54 and 3/4 winters
have whitened me
ever so gradually
can I say
I love this being
who has
accreted cell by cell
from that one small zygote
sprouted arms and legs
and lungs and heart
then crawled and walked
and lunged full bore
into childhood
then adolescence
then womanhood?

can I say I love this
strange
compelling creature
who moves me
expresses me
is me?

yes,
I can say the words
I love you
to myself
but do I hear them?
do I heed them?

do they penetrate
the hidden corners
of doubt and dark
to bring nourishment
to all that comprises
this blink of self?

for the first time
I believe
the answer
may be
yes

it was not easy infatuation
not love at first sight

the bond has grown slowly
like an arranged marriage
ripening into caring
and commitment
but I can say it now
after 54 and 3/4 years

I can whisper it
into my own ear
with tenderness
newly found
and it rings
finally
with abiding truth

Brinksmanship

I balance on
a thin black line
drawn without waver
by time
I slide along
without grace
eyes fixed ahead
on a stationary point
a tipping point

I am a woman on the brink
children leaving home
youth leaving body
memory leaving mind
yet still I balance
avoiding the plummet
teetering between nostalgia
and inexplicable thrill

I walk the straight line
between now and next
moving erect and ready
breathing steady
looking forward
instead of down
into the
possible futures
below

I move my feet with care
no skipping, no tripping
just deliberate care
each step conscious
and inexorable

I am on the cusp
of molting
shedding old skins of
tending and rearing
before sliding forth
with fresh color

but for now I balance
on the edge
of known and unknown
trying to prolong the hiatus
trying to dodge evolution
trying to delay the plunge
from the present's high wire
into the waiting arms of
my future self

Habits and Habitats of Truth

sometimes
when my truth lies buried
I catch glimpses of
its sapphire sparkle
its golden glint
shining from beneath
brown leaf litter
and I relish the dirt
jamming under my nails
as I excavate what I know

sometimes
when my truth is quiet
not sulking in silence
just watching with no need
to shout its presence
I must become
still and soft as new snow
to hear its
refreshing voice

at times
when my truth lies dormant
nesting in its cocoon
while metamorphosis
liquefies its form
I summon patience
knowing if I rip
the silken shield
in desperation to know
it will wither
without transforming
into new relevance

my truth is my soul sister
shadowing my journey
in the world's bright light
she is my dark companion
who whispers
in dreams and portents
and guides me
through nudges and hints
toward home
always toward home

That One Thing

you wait
for that one thing
you wait
squinting to catch
your true self
ghosting the mirror
your purpose
shimmering in the desert
your passion
singing like a siren
you wait
searching in your heart
as though rifling
through a purse
for the keys
to the kingdom
you wait
as coffee cups empty
as hair bleeds out its color
as children grow up and leave
you wait
without knowing
that the act of waiting
makes it recede
the passive expectation
the critical evaluation
the impatient denigration
all scare it away
if you desire it
you must
welcome
rather than wait
you must
open the door
to that one thing
embracing it like a lost twin
inviting it in to share
champagne and crudités

celebrating the reunion
as it gets comfy on your couch
where it has
resided all along

My Havens Are...

family
the hugs and hellos
sighs and supplications of
four people turning around
the hub of heart
like spokes on a wheel

silence
the sacred space of aloneness
sun fingering through the window
comma of black cat on a couch
diaphanous steam ghosting from tea
my thoughts roaming free

writing
dancing with words
twisting and dipping
dripping sweat as we spin
trading intimacies as we
tango across the page

nature
robins eavesdropping on worms
beetles marching like armored tanks
droplets of dew beading nasturtiums
buds pregnant with dogwood blossoms
poppy petals opening like prayers

connection
eyes meeting and lingering
seeing and being seen
hands knowing when to comfort
and when to fold away
bestowing room to be

soul
the place at the center of myself
where essence hums
and spirit sings
strong and clear

Held

I was alone in a house
with night-blackened windows
reflecting a phantom self

it echoed with
long-gone children
laughing, crying
suffering micro-traumas
yet opening
like magnolia buds
into plump perfection

it flowed with
remnants of currents
from a marriage maturing
over thirty-some years
of union and separation
like a braided river

I was alone in a house
devoid of the pulse of others
not even a cat to offer
a purr of presence
alone with
my fingers
my toes
my too-loud heart
my sedimentary memories
deposited in layers of time

I was alone
thinking my thoughts
feeling my centrality
in my own story
inhabiting my perspective
as I must

I was alone
feeling my atoms spin
through the space within
as I spun through
the cosmos without
I was alone
yet I felt orbited
by children, family, friends
while orbiting others in turn
and I could sense
overlapping patterns
of stand-alone specks
inhabiting the vastness
together

I felt as if
threads of silk
weightless
insubstantial
but with enormous
tensile strength
bound me to my tribe

I was alone
but held
in a heart-string web
vibrating
along with others

I was alone
but held

Nesting

an owl carved by a craftsman's hand
in some far-flung land
carries a smaller owl
nesting in its belly
just barely visible
through a lacy latticework
of hand-hewn wood
a mystery held within

everything contains within it
seeds of something smaller
diminishing multitudes
reducing
to the world
of atoms
and finally
empty space
blessed empty space
out of which news things grow

I feel nested within me
figurines of former selves

just below my current skin
of writer and coach
shimmers the young mother
turned inward with love
her nest is her world
and her chicks fill her vision
she has eyes for nothing else

that self holds within her
the consultant sporting
broad-shouldered suits
and uncomfortable pumps
playing the game
wearing the masks

masquerading as a
professional at the peak
of her career

within her dwells
the free-spirited adventurer
the rebel girl with flowered hair
chasing true love and magic
across the continent's
wrinkled face

within that one crouches
the boarding school student
moving without mooring
or navigational aids
sailing the seas
of adolescence alone
among multitudes
of ostensible peers

within her skips
the girl with crooked bangs
gap-toothed grin
and algae-laced hair
skin tanned and sweat-crusty
from the shores of Lake Erie
embracing the promise
of unsupervised summer

within her lies
the small one
curled with a book
stuffed animals
and playmates created
from thin air
hoping
hoping to be asked to play
by brothers who tower
like redwoods

and within that one rests
the infant
and within the infant lies
the womb-dwelling prototype
and within that small clump of cells lies
whatever was before
a spark of spirit
lighting the dark energy
of atomic space
the empty fullness
out of which
everything
is carved

Negative Sound

what we do not say creates phantoms
that ghost our peripheral vision
mirages that shimmer
just beyond sight
silent symphonies
that echo unheard in our bones

what we fail to speak
is spoken anyway
through eyes averted or met
over Saturday pancakes
through hands clasped or avoided
during Sunday walks

what we stifle
seeps out anyway
from the back turned away
in the too big bed
from the mute grimace
of denying mouths

what we swallow into silence
becomes carnivorous
consuming our soft parts
leaving ribs cages devoid of heart
and graying pelvises
leached of passion

but when we give voice to our shame
when we stutter our hurt to another
or croak out a *no* or *yes*
that needs to be freed
when we risk exposing
the buried yearning
life force
flows

Happenstance

you let it happen

you let the poetry of love
turn into
a leaden prose of mistakes
where jagged words
were hurled from
injured hearts

you let the
sugar coating of care
be stripped bare
leaving only drab regret
and the skeletal remains
of spent coupling

how did you squander
the blood and treasure
you amassed together?

how did you eat
each other up
so completely
that nothing was left
but love's faded skin?

don't let it happen

shout into the past
to the pivot point
follow that one thin vein
that still dribbles with life
to its beating core

resuscitate that
withered thing
whatever it takes
thump it into pumping
with feeling again

notice wisps of new breath
beginning to stir the air
don't turn away

you can make it happen

let the poetry of communion
move your tongue
fill your lips with
heart-blood wine

open your
dammed self
and fight for what
is wasting away
as though it was
your
last
precious
child

begin again
with six words

I
am
sorry
I
love
you

Wanting

wanting creates its own momentum until
the wanting becomes more compelling
than the wanted
we reach, we yearn, we grasp
contorting in supplication
letting life idle while we run
toward vapors and mists that seem
truer than the cereal crumbs
on our child's face
the snow of dandruff on
our spouse's pillow
the crumpled calendar pages
numbering our days

wanting is a master of sleight-of-hand
now you see it, now you don't
as the lusted-after dream
fades into a hoarse whisper
then falls silent altogether and
the remains of wanting
seem spent, gray, used up
compared to the luster of fantasy

it takes time to refocus on
what our animal body knows
the low tones in our child's laugh
the way our partner offers mint tea
the crystal chill of orange dawn

it takes attention to notice
the chickadee tapping the window
in search of a mate
the quince blossoms opening white
then deepening to coral
the cat's lick feeling
soft and barbed at the same time

slowly we re-acclimate to the real
as the spell of wanting loses its power
to ensnare and command us
and someday
we may find that
the end of wanting
is the start of peace

Beginning

begin to wonder how beginning
becomes momentum
how you muster the courage
to take that first step
to lift your foot curled in protective leather
and put it down in new territory
never before touched
by your particular sole

after enduring that ordeal
you go on to risk another step
on the heels of your first attempt
this time your foot lands
with greater assurance
you spring forward off your toes
with optimism building
and a sense of destiny unfurling

pretty soon you pick up speed
arms swinging freely
and feet striding purposefully
you sidestep tripping hazards with finesse
feeling momentum, grace, and strength
you create an anything-is-possible gait
that parts sidewalk crowds
and conveys you are someone
who is clearly going somewhere

but eventually
when your head is held so high
that you can't see the ground
you step off an unseen edge
free-fall for a few astounded seconds
and come down hard
in front of onlookers
lying sullied
by the grime of the daily grind
as your momentum dribbles away

but you can't stay down forever
so with legs squatting and butt jutting
you rise up from the earth
once again thinking about beginning
wondering if you dare start over
if you can bear the knowledge that
whenever you hit a new stride
another ledge will eventually appear

you stand for a while
looking at the Canada geese
V-ing overhead in purposeful flight
you smile at the concerned taco vendor
offering a jalapeno hand of help just in case

you notice mica flecks
glinting in the concrete like jewels
and the first surge of *maybe*
grows into a force of *yes*
igniting will in your raw heart
yoking brain to nerve to sinew
until your leg rises of its own accord
and you begin to start anew

Ageless Writer

you see me as a wizened woman
with clawed hands
clutching her coat

you see mottled skin
with lacey blue veins
hanging off bones

you see sunken eyes
with drooping lids
clouded with confusion

what you see
is a mirage of age
shimmering in front of essence

I am mother, daughter
sister, lover, writer
always writer

I am tender-sprouted toddler
almost-ripened teen
fully-fruited woman

I am smooth-skinned youth
stretched tight
beneath sham decay

I hear whirlwinds of words
at night
when sleep feints and jabs

I pulse with fierce passions
to write
in spite of crabbed hands

you see desiccation
I feel fertile phrases
rooting in black loam

you see decline
I feel survival
pounding in my heart

you see doddering
I feel rage
roaring at my irrelevance

let my word swords
slash the invisibility
cloaking me and choking me

let me tell you a story
that beguiles you into becoming
an ashtray, an orphan, an insect

let me show you
that you are me and
everyone and everything

you will see me
as a word weaver
creating infinite worlds

you will see me
as a story spinner
cocooning you in her web

you will see me
as an ageless writer
wielding the power to enchant

you *will* see me

A Thought

I had a thought
that thoughts are made of nothing
just puffs of electrical impulses
blowing along dendritic paths
as evanescent and invisible
as breezes stirring the trees
then dying out to stillness

I realized that
thinking
leads to feeling and wanting
which leads to acting
which changes everything
and yet
the causes
of both our dire strife
and our stunning achievement
are mere figments
of our imaginations

thoughts
arise and disappear
like clouds sauntering
across an impassive sky
but they have a strange habit
of manifesting
as murder and mayhem
and healing and beauty
and everything in between
somehow
becoming something real
buildings and spaceships
bombs and weapons
dances and poems
all spun
from the same
stuff of
nothing

Flight Feather

the feather was broken
quill bent
at right angles
standing at half mast
like my brain
so recently concussed
and whacked perpendicular
to itself

the hawk couldn't fly
nor could my mind
swollen with bruises
wiped clean of words
grounded and slogging
with the muteness of
bird-brained thought

the feather was dropped
when the bird shed her
broken thing
just as I had to shed
much of who
I took myself to be

layers of identity
lay like discarded feathers
scattered around
my earth-bound feet

talking
thinking
doing
deciding
organizing
planning
connecting
giving
all these fell from me

now I get to choose
which aspects
of personality
to reclaim
and which to leave
on the ground
to molder

new feathers
are sprouting
and itching to feel
the rush of air

I preen them with
careful gratitude
hoping that I might
fly again

soon a breeze
will catch me
lift me
above the dense
ground fog
up and up
in slow motion
spiraling
towards the clarity
of sun
the movement
of clouds
the vision
of raptors

I trust that
the soft strength
of my new
flight feathers
will help me
rise again

Waiting World

the worn pieces of the past
cling like shreds of snake skin
as I try to molt my way into
into whatever is next

my mind clings to the
life I've outgrown
wanting
the bustle
the busy
the get-it-done satisfaction
of my old driven self

but my bruised brain
howls
no
and
can't
and
not that way

then my soul offers
an alternative
something fresh
and juicy
like a just-cut mango
presented in orange crescents
on an emerald banana leaf
full of scent
full of sun
full of now

I am shown
that the known way
of habit and ego
of excess and success
of navigation by to-do list
no longer fits my expanding self
that space and silence
are where invitation lies

I am offered a chance
to slip between the cracks
of what I have constructed
and the formerly solid structure
made to last a lifetime
now yields to a gentle push

I step into vibrancy and vitality
into pulsing color and radiant movement
into life force and spirit dance
into the immediacy of being
and at least
for a moment
I glimpse
the waiting world

The Practice

daily I fall in love with
the blades of grass and maple leaves
gobbling the sun
sending liquid cruising through
phloem and xylem highways

daily I fall in love with
the brushes that paint the clouds
and stir them to motion
Japanese calligraphy
at its most sublime

daily I fall in love with
my own quirky, persistent body
my flawed and aging face
that still sparks from the eyes
my organs churning and producing
like an automated factory

daily I fall in love with
my creative impulses
the writing, the thinking, the serving
the making of food, art, and relationships
the two new human beings I have
seeded upon the earth

daily I fall in love with feeling
the surges of sadness
the knee buckling grief
the longing for what was
the flashes of warrior anger
the soft gladness
the melting thankfulness
the spurts of festive exuberance
that are my humanity

daily I fall in love with
my ability to fall in love
to choose optimism, appreciation
and responsibility for my creations
rather than blame and victimhood

daily I fall in love with
the ecstasy of beauty
the fiesta that is color
the textures, patterns
shadings and illuminations
that bring feasts to my eyes

daily I fall in love with
my place in it all
sister to the grass blades
the maple leaves
those who creep and leap and fly
and my fellow humans
bursting with shame and glory
as they struggle alongside me
to crawl out of the muck
and into the light

Message from the Oracle

the space between words
is where
breath happens

the space between thoughts
is where
awareness dawns

the space between moments
is where
presence dwells

find the gaps
step in
and expand

let identity
release its grip
in stillness

let consciousness
shift forms
as it manifests

rest
in the
self
beyond
words

and the
silence
from
which
words
flow

Elements

Portrait

begin my portrait
with browns and greens
and rich blood reds
at the bottom of the scene

cushion my feet
with mosses and ferns
let streams lap my toes
and vines wrap my legs

lady bugs and scarabs
are welcome on my skin
snakes and salamanders
may S around my feet

add fairy slipper orchids
in delicate detail
and a hint of magic
to the yellow light

in the background
paint a stag
with prodding antlers
and white-flag tail

add a brown bear
with curved claws
reaching forward
for embrace

from the waist up
erase the earthen tones
drape me with vibrant silks
and weave bluets into my curls

wind sapphire, lapis, tanzanite
around my singing throat
let an emerald pendant dangle
just above my heart

near my head
paint a hummingbird buzzing
through extravagant rainbows
add a crown of gold and amethyst
to open me to god
then sketch a snowy owl
blending with my sky

next fill in
with tender care
the blank space
of my face

for eyes, opals
that lead to other worlds
for mouth, an ocean
licking the salty shore

now paint me a body
vital and robust

for hands
give me maple leaves
with fringed fingers
translucent in the sun

for breasts
give me Rocky Mountains
iced white with snow

for legs
give me redwoods
shaggy with soft bark

tattoo in blue my family
onto my sensitive skin
inscribe me with their names
to show I am
marked by love

then when you're done
when you've captured me
light it

light it
all
on
fire

Teenage Transcendence

at sixteen, I believed in
soul flight and moonlight
I sensed subterranean rivers
raging beneath my feet
I saw strings
of time and space
weaving a shimmering fabric
as I balanced
exhilarated
in my own
precarious moment

I heard the buzz
of vitality in leaves
and felt phloem and xylem
surging with liquid life
I osmosed inky silhouettes
of geese taking off at sunset
I knew I flew with them
and they rested in me
transcendentally

I believed in
my power
to conjure the invisible
to materialize beauty
from the thick stuff of creation
to entice others to blast walls and lids
off the boxes that contained them

at sixteen, I believed in
effervescent sun
and undulating shadow
more than dirt and bones

now I look for solid footing
on fertile ground
and I stand
rooted

but with eyes
still cast
toward
the clouds

Erie Elements

Lake Erie weather
weathered me
into my current form

snow flurries
streaking white and
slashing eyelashes

slushy slurries
of crystalline mud
sloshing into boot tops

slanted rain furies
piercing exposed skin
with watery needles

glowering clouds
hiding the cowering
weak-willed sun

ice storms
making crystalline forms
and jagged diamond daggers

wind chill
chilling marrow and
freezing breathing lungs

ice caves
of frozen waves
sheltering daredevil teens

snowdrifts
shifting and blowing
like crawling desert dunes

pipkrakes
raking the earth
with tiny icy tines

wonders of thunder
rattling windows
with *basso profundo* booms

lightning
enlightening
thickly forested nights

water spouts
twisting mist
over the leaden lake

towering waves
devouring and scouring
leaving shorelines purged

columnar curtains of rain
racing over water
stippling its skin

metallic colors of winter
zinc, aluminum, steel
plating the landscape gray

yellow rays of spring
gilding crocus tips and
kissing forsythia lips

thickened air of summer
pressing and distressing
with hot, heavy, humidity

dripping drizzle
dulling and culling
the flame of autumn leaves

Erie weather
ruled and shaped me
with imperious
impetuous
will

Facets

I am an azurite geode
plain on the outside
with a glittering crystalline core

I am an Anna's hummingbird
flashing my gem throat
and searching for drinkable color

I am a she-grizzly
feeling sun on my shaggy pelt
while nosing for salmon and blueberries

I am a whip snake shedding her skin
slithering into transformation by
risking rawness

I am a calypso orchid
flowering magenta with speckles
beneath redwoods and ferns

I am a word-based life form
with language for blood
and expression for breath

I am a weaver
reaching for threads
to create communal tapestries

I am a healer
with burning hands
and smoking knowledge

I am a very specific mother
and the archetypal mother
feeling the ancient womb-pull

I am kaleidoscopic patterns
and ever-changing reflections
of the infinitely faceted
I Am

Baptism

the rain slinks down my back
oozes off my chin
drips down my cleavage
and pools in my navel
like mercury

it is intimate
a caress from the sky
arms open
mouth open
my tongue catches the wet gift
that runs from my hair in rivulets

my toes dig into cool sand
seeking the sun-warmed layer
pausing there enrobed in silica
while waves surge against the shore
sporting white collars of lace

my own water whispers
with the shushing rain and waves
my own tides pulse with the moon
my own tears flow like the cloud's
I am bathed and baptized by this shower

I slip into the ocean
a reverse birth
immersed in salt water
washed with fresh water
knowing I am
home

Snake

I wade waist-deep
naked as Eve
into a crystalline pool
just as snake's
tear-drop head
juts from rocks
beside a cascade

I stand eye-to-eye
with a quiet miracle
so close I can see
the cleft in her tongue
as she tastes my air

I speak to her
and still she stays
listening impassively

I move closer and
still she stays
weaving her head
side to side
inches from my face

I move even closer
and still she stays
teaching me
slender agility
brazen confidence and
the faith necessary
to shed skin
and become new

I pull back first
then she disappears
into the
cool
dark
crack

of her own
unfathomable
mystery

The Women in the Moon

the moon
is white
like the teeth
of the goddess
in smile or snarl

half her face
is shadow-veiled
the other shows her
pockmarked skin
glaring with naked clarity

she wears no rouge
to beguile us
and is harshly
blatantly
herself

she pulls
at our wombs
until we pour forth
blood tribute

she hunts what is
hidden in our hearts
stalking us through
forests of dreams

she irradiates
the underbelly of
our waking world
revealing strangeness
with a mercury glow

you and I are the
women in the moon
arcing and rotating
waxing and waning

my shadow calls
to your luminosity
your darkness dances
with my light

To Fledge a Friendship

lay an egg from
a hopeful heart
cup it in your
warm, pulsing hands
offer it to her
gently, protectively
so her hands too
can shelter
potential life

pass the perfect ovoid
back and forth
between you
from woman hand
to woman hand
from womanhood
to womanhood

the two of you
will mother this
pale blue possibility
until it hatches
and runs chirping
in circles
on tiny, bony feet

then you will know
how fragile
yet robust
is this new being
you have incubated
into existence

it will imprint
on you both
grow pin feathers
then flight feathers
hop and flap
until it soars

from you to her
from her to you
migrating
according to need
over unspooling time

Complete

the old woman sits in stillness
her skin a riverbed
cracked from drought
and dried to crumbling

her eyes are apertures
letting light out
her vision a sculptor's tool
removing the extraneous

her mouth is quiet
content with having told
stories to last
beyond a lifetime

her stomach rests
done with its wanting
hunger lulled by lullabies
and nourishment taken from light

her womb is empty
but the echoes of creation
still reverberate
through its mute redness

her heart is purring
not pounding
softly murmuring
I still love, I still love, I still love

her mind has spread out
wide as the cosmos
roving diffuse and free
through truth beyond time

her lungs sip air
one dainty taste at a time
savoring each
like the last morsel
of a delectable dessert

Small Things

my mother gave me
the aquamarine ring
she lost and re-found
as an unbound girl
but my cavalier trust
in my capacity to keep
collapsed inward
when I lost
that full-circle ring

losing small things
can feel vast

the cell clump
wedged in my fallopian tube
was striving to become human
but I lost that seed of potential
and the future fantasies
curled tightly at its core
when the surgeon found it
with her stainless tools

losing small things
can feel vast

after becoming a mother at last
I dreamed of my new baby
shrinking then vanishing
in a mound of junk
I pawed through the pile
only to find
a blank-staring doll
of rigid pink rubber
at the bottom of the heap

losing small things
can feel vast

in the baggage claim
I looked up to see nothing
where my toddler used to sit
when I bellowed her name
once, twice, thrice
she emerged from behind
the amenities map
alarmed by
my panicked call

losing small things
can feel vast

my grown children on cue
caught the breeze in their sails
and tacked away from my shore
I waved until
their specks disappeared
into the hungry horizon

losing small things
can feel vast

a massive limb of the grandmother oak
cracked and was cleft from her trunk
but she whispered
loss can be lightening too
if you let earth support you
while reaching for the sun

finding small things
can feel vast

Flower Envy

I want to bloom with brilliance
like a firecracker penstemon
exploding with crimson trumpets

I want to herald the spring as
a beacon for hummingbirds
iridescently sipping and supping

I want to feel my tiny taproots
searching the soil while
my germ uncoils in a spiral dance

I want to see my paleness
saturating into chartreuse
as the sun warms my soil

I want to feel the excitement
of my first leaves unfurling
their small but mighty fists

I want to know the suspense
of my tight buds opening
in a revelation of color

I want to taste sweet nectar
syruping my petals and
beckoning in the bugs

I want to know the drone of bees
and the tickle of velvet bellies
soft against my own

I want to reach skyward with
earthworms weaving
their wetness between my toes

I want to feel the sacred vocation
of growing new seeds
in the midst of my own decay

Taking Nourishment

swallow the sun
bring that fiery orb
into the belly of the beast
that is you
feel its warmth radiating
into sinew and cell
bone and brain
let the hot light
burn away
what's extraneous
let it melt you
so you can flow
like molten bronze
within the crucible
of your skin

swallow the shadow too
gulp the purple coolness
like water from
an underground spring
let it flow through your
soft pulp
cleansing and blessing
your shame and fear
feel its blue-black fingers
soothing inflamed places
and refreshing parched parts
that have thirsted

ingest and digest
sun and shadow both
let them swirl together
inside you
in the eternal dance
of light and dark
out of which all has risen

for blesséd are both

Reading the Rubble

in the wake of flood or fire
tornado or tsunami
the thing that sears
is the vacant stare of
a tattered doll

your eyes roam over
steeples torn from churches
single shoes crumpled
with tongues lolling
couches stranded
with crows in tree tops
pages of books
swirling like ghost breath

your eyes search for signs of life
some heroic blades of green
the flit of blue butterflies
a family bereft but intact

your eyes search for signs of death
dogs crushed under bent porches
the remains of ornery homesteaders
buried *in situ* by choice

but your eyes stop their sweep
startled, horrified
when they glimpse
pink plastic doll flesh
now muddied and gray
tiny grasping hands
mimicking the reach toward hope
belly rounded
as though brimming with milk
pudgy legs frozen
in ripeness for toddling
cornflower blue eyes
still somehow innocent
of destruction and decay

you know a small girl
once held this doll
diapered it
dressed it
whispered it
soft endearments
don't cry baby
don't cry
mama's got you
you're safe and sound
everything's okay now

you can feel that girl's presence
in her first-day-of-school dress
you can see her brown hair
pulled tight in cascading braids
you can see her trying to walk
with purpose like her mother
you can see her pushing a doll stroller
as though on her way for groceries

you see her and feel her
even though
no trace of her remains
except the pink doll
made of indestructible
petroleum products
able to withstand
acts of god

Blind Spots

I glance at the high-noon sun
rebel that I am
and its dark twin
dances on my retina
obscuring my vision
with Rorschach ink blots

I sit in the hot tub
under a new moon
staring at the faint glow
around the edges
of the blotted out orb
contemplating
the black navel
in the belly of night

I watch the solar eclipse
through pin-hole projections
on blank white paper
the fiery fixture
dwindling to a crescent
then becoming
a mere memory
invoked by a shadow

like the eye and the sky
the heart and the mind
are host to blind spots
erased places
leaving negative spaces
where a lover, a friend
a parent, a pet
a trauma, a triumph
once dwelled

sometimes
the blanked slate is merciful
allowing hope to regrow
in a field of devastation
when seeing is too painful
and blindness becomes
survival's weapon

other times the deletion
is torment
when we seek
without finding
the voice
the smell
the smile
of one who has faded
from physical form

in spite of it all
I open my eyes
and look to the sky
for illumination
choosing
to be blind
to the coming
of darkness

The Plunge

grief
you bottomless abyss
containing
shell-shocked whales
liquefied starfish
drowning polar bears
extinct things
and soon-to-be extinct things
climbing temperatures
receding ice
starving children
war-driven refugees
earthquake victims
fire survivors
abused innocents
and personal sorrows
regarding friends and family
dreams and fantasies
time that can never be reclaimed
and losses yet to come

normally
I can dip my toe in
then turn away
with Protestant composure
still intact

but yesterday
you said come on in
the water's fine
and uncharacteristically
I dove in
hoping
I would not be
sucked down
beyond breath
beyond light
beyond redemption

I feared the submersion
I feared the letting go
necessary to be cleansed
but surprisingly
others were with me
in the quicksilver depths
I saw a hand reaching out
felt the brush of a kiss
and heard undulating waves
of keening
that let me know
I was not alone

I came up for air
three times
allowing myself to
surface and sink
surface sink
surface and sink
until finally
I felt the pull
of light and land
the calm
of emptied tears
and the peace
of a baptized heart

Evolution

something will happen
any minute now
it always does
pebbles will plunge
ponds will ripple
butterfly wings will stir winds
across the globe

any minute now
we will blossom
tight buds
of potential unfurling
into profusions of petals
the hue and aroma
our very own

any minute now
we will erupt ecstatically
magma from our interior
spilling down our sides
illuminating the night
with sparks and ropes
of fiery light

any minute now
we will begin dancing
rumba, mambo
samba, tango
dipping, swirling
fast feet drumming
a rhythm of awakening

any minute now
we will all play together
each instrument and melody
weaving harmonies
in synchronic symphony
with no conductor needed
to spray music across the sky

Marrow

The Oddities of Bodies

how strange
these things that
house our fleeting spirits
carry our rarified minds
shelter our earnest hearts

these bodies
festooned with
fingers, penises
ears, scrotums
noses, labias
elbows, clitorises

and adorned with
pelts in sundry places
armpits, faces
crotches, scalps
buttocks, legs

these bodies
specialized for sex
boasting their own
custom-crafted
curves and valleys
sculpted with
protrusions and inclusions
to propagate
the species

who's to say
which is more beautiful?
the blush of nipple
on heavy breast
or the flat firmness
of furred chest?
the proud display
of phallus
or the sacred sheltering
of vagina?

how peculiar
these bodies
their attractions
their drives
their longings
and crazy capabilities

how odd
the flaps of flesh
that make the ear
curl inward
like a chambered shell
and the nose
cleave the air
like a cartilaginous scalpel
and the toes in a row
grip onto the earth
like vestigial fingers

and the eyeball
for god's sake
swiveling jelly-filled
in its socket
and the convoluted navel
lying naked in
the belly's expanse
like an imprint
of the kiss of life

these bodies
so appalling
and so sublime
so full of
delicate precision
and embarrassing excess

how strange
these bodies
so miraculous
yet utterly mundane
as they
strive to survive
and replicate
themselves
ad infinitum

Blue Marble

what about that imperceptible scar
deep inside?
what about the hair-thin incision
traced on my fallopian tube
and the hard blue marble
the surgeon liberated from its crypt?
what about the ghost of might-have-been?
what about expectation and culmination
and having told everyone
in grand celebration
we had finally conceived?

what about seeing the first blood
and returning home
from LA for a D&C
to lie alone on a cold steel table
having refused
my husband's offer
of compassion, of company?
what about not wanting him
to miss the beat of work
while I lost the pulse of pregnancy?
what about the sobs that came
like a roiling boil from my depths
as I lay there splayed and flayed?
what about entering
my storybook Victorian
emptied of hope and offspring?

what about the next time
afraid to claim the new pregnancy
knowing it could all collapse
into a figment of fantasy?
what about feeling my daughter quicken
undeniably in my womb
and striving to believe
in the possibility
of her continued existence?

what about knowing she
passed through that fallopian tube
mute and blind to its history
before pushing down the birth canal
insistent on her own life?

what about when I dreamed
I dropped her
and she disintegrated
into smaller and smaller bits
finally scattering
like ashes on the wind
and disappearing
like the idea-child before her?

what about hidden scars
(nothing to see, move along folks)?
what about those
invisible fractures and fault lines
connected to the
deepest ruptures
in our world?

what about that blue sphere
looking like our precious earth
when viewed from the
sterile vastness of space?

what about that?

Daisy Moments

your petals are serrated
like a first grader's front teeth
your center stares
like a yellow eye
you ask a koan query
in a spring-breeze voice

where are the lost moments?

daughter's legs plump like sausages
sun-smell in springy ringlets
Buddha belly burnished to a sheen
goodbye tears at day care
fairies in ferns and fens
pigtails curled like poodle ears

where are those petals now?

son's hair like milkweed silk
love of exhaust pipes and down spouts
mind asking how and why
ecstatic with zoom and vroom
fingers fiddling and fidgeting
soft hand holding on tight

where are those petals now?

I plucked the moments
one by one
let them flutter away
like wind-blown seeds
now I sift through soil
searching for what's lost
in the dream-filled mulch
of undifferentiated love

Fountains

my son made fountains
not recognizable burbling ones
but intricate sculptures
from mangled slabs
of technicolor clays
stacked into precarious
curvilinear towers

he appeared often
hands behind his back singing
navy navy nick nack
which hand do you tick tack
then out came his masterpiece
presented with
the reverence of a relic

I made you a fountain
he said
blue eyes shining with pride
let me show how it works
he said
fine blond hair
brushing my cheek
and four-year-old aroma
of dirt and baby shampoo
filling my senses

here's where the water comes out
and here's the pump for circulation
and here's the overflow drain
in case there's too much water
and . . .

he saw every detail
of his fantasy fountain
he saw perfection
function
and precise engineering
accomplished
by his own small hands

I saw writhing color
imagination
and attention to detail
demonstrating his desire
to make meaning and beauty

thank you, honey
I love my fountain
I said time after time

thank you, buddy
I love my fountain
my husband said time after time

he put earthquake clay
on the bottom of one
stuck it to his dashboard
and drove around with the
fountain leading the way

now my son's gifts
are words and deeds
of caring and sensitivity

but they are still fountains
beneath it all
ever renewing
ever flowing
fresh as water

Z Power

two men
one becoming
one already arrived
pool genes, minds, and bodies
to restore a car to glorious luster

father and son
tinker and putter
twist and torque
speaking lingo
strange to outside ears
words like
brake caliper, zirk head, honing gun
rolling off testosterone tongues

they tighten bonds
while they tighten screws
gods breathing life into creation
using faith and miracles
to resurrect a dead Datsun 240 Z

their tall slender frames
glide beneath a sapphire blue one
cushioned on castored creepers
they know the intimate rub
of flesh belly against metal belly

these two men say nothing
of heartache or revelation
the texture of talk
is rational and analytical
poetry pulsing only
in the mechanical words
that careen between them

but something ineffable
happens under the hood
they merge through
hand and mind engagement

anticipating each other's thoughts
offering a wrench before requested
moving as one to hoist the engine
clad in matching mechanics' shirts

they proudly proclaim themselves
gearheads, part jockeys, grease monkeys
and find fellow tribesmen
in garages across the land
they earn clan membership
through rust-removal rituals
and initiation rites of calculating
probable rpms and engine drag

these two are building more than a car
they are renovating their connection
to reflect the incipient manhood of one
and the mid-age settle of the other
they are redefining father and son

they are celebrating
the power of their pistons
while cackling about
lube jobs, short shafts, ball joints
and exchanging insider jokes

for father and son
each tender caress of the Z's sleek body
speaks of who they are to each other
and what it means to work together

the car is the vehicle
for male bonding
of the most sacramental sort
Z power and Z glory
forever and ever
ah . . . men

Separating

the taste of tears is with me
while visiting my daughter at college
tears ever-ready but never shed
create a mirage that
distorts the shape of my baby
into the figment of a young woman

these tears threaten
to breech the sea wall
but I push them back
because she needs
celebration not heartache
liberation not longing
lightness not the weight of a mother
trying to release her child into the world

salty wavelets lap against my lids
then recede like an ebbing tide
only to surge when our eyes
suddenly meet and hold
blue merging with blue

the resolute cheerfulness
freezes on our faces
dissolving with no words
to make it stop hurting
even 'I love you'
becoming irrelevant
because it can only hint
at the blurring
shimmering truth

in that moment
before she plunges back
into the swirling currents
of her new life
I realize
the juice of the heart
is salty like tears
and she tastes it too

Mother's Marrow

I can't protect my daughter
I can't save her from mistakes
I can't do what my mother's marrow
is programmed to do

I want to snatch her
from the sharp-toothed
maw of danger
as a mother bear
would defend her cub
haul her from quicksand
with the adrenaline-fueled strength
of all ancestral mothers combined
pin her to the earth
with the weight of my love
so avalanches and floods
can't sweep her away

I want to shout
with lungs powerful enough
to resound throughout the cosmos
YOU MAY NOT HURT MY BABY!

but I can't

instead of power
I must feel my smallness
my inability to intervene
in a life that is
bursting out of old confines
and expanding beyond my reach

I must sit humbled by this miracle
set in motion nineteen years ago
surrender my illusion of omnipotence
for the reality of impotence
ingest faith and trust like comfort food
to sustain me through the renovation
of this primal bond

if only she could be small again
I could hold her tiny hand
and keep her safe
at least while crossing the road
but now the road leads her away
far beyond my force-field

my heart flutters after her
a feather-light moth
seeking to reach her
but being blown astray
by a capricious breeze

Which Came First?

they have fledged
I felt the air
stirred by their wing beats
watched the sky swallow
their receding forms

and now
more than the chicks have gone
the twigs have crumbled
the dried droppings
have become blowing dust
the downy lining
has disintegrated too

I am left in a vessel
with smooth porcelain walls
I can't grab on
can't get traction
to scramble up
one curved side or the other
can't find an edge to peer over
to see beyond
the harsh whiteness
the soothing blandness
that surrounds me
blinds me
becalms me

and here I'll rest
curving my body
to the barren walls
mother dissolving
into embryo
protected by
the thinnest shell
from being crushed
by the weight of loss

until my new form
solidifies and strengthens
enough
to crack free

The Heart of the Matter

what I really want to say is
come back to me
sweet children
sweet past
where you snuggled close
and let me be
your whole world

I want to say
let me inhale you
caress you
feel you melt into mama-love
so I can know
my essentialness
in my very bones

what I really want to say is
please give me both *now* and *then*
both the easy camaraderie
of interacting as grown people
with lives of our own
and the blessed cocoon
of interdependence
we knew when our
hearts beat in sync

help me find an outlet for this love
that is bigger than us all
help me not tamp it down
and act as though my love
isn't bursting its bonds
and threatening to
sweep us away

what I really want to say is
let me love you
let me find meaning in that love
let me still be your mama
please

just let me still
be your
mama

Containers

ghosts of former contents
linger and waft
in empty jars
that once held
raw almonds
shaped like tears
and sour cherries
bursting with tart

currently
the jars stand empty
at the ready
for repurposing
willing
to be drafted
for new missions

right now they are
filled with nothing
holding only
insubstantial air
like lungs waiting
to exhale
so they can take in
new breath

I feel like a container
spilling my last crumbs
leaking stale elixirs
dribbling toward
the hollow echo
of emptiness

but I am not fragile
in danger of shattering
like brittle glass
I am not rigid
built only for
form and function

a time will come
when I will find
new purpose

I am more than mother

I have my own
ineffable essence
swirling in the space
where children
used to fill me
to the brim

I hold and am held
I am both
container and contents
flowing and filling
spilling and refilling

I am more
than mother

Inexorable Change

untamed change moves over me
like a glacial monolith
holding eons of ice
oozing downslope
with black-hole density

I am scoured
and scraped
sculpted
and shaped
beneath its forward force

my heart freezes
with fight or flight
but you can't outrun a glacier
when pinned
under its icy weight

so I try to relax
under the dark grind
inhale the uncaring coldness
allow myself to be
scrubbed clean
created anew

I accept parts will be
snapped off
cracked through
tumbled and polished
in glacial embrace
then dumped in a
new terrain of foreign moraines

but my crystalline components
will remain the same
whether in jagged cliffs
rounded boulders
or sandy soil grains

so I'll let the frozen
impersonal river
mold me in the quiet cold
waiting to see what shape I'll be
when the force moves
beyond me

Penance

I want to sink quietly with you
into the watery peace
where striving and pushing
ease into swimming and floating

I want to strip away
your warrior's chain mail
and hold your pain
like a madonna cradling a babe

I'm sorry
for the words
that have lodged in your heart
like twisting foxtails

I'm sorry
for the panic that
drags you down
like stone-filled pockets

I'm sorry
for the messages of little faith
that chisel away at your
fighting spirit

let me offer my penance
so you can
redeem us both
with your healing

Apologies

no apologies
necessary
you say
yet how can I
release regret before
being absolved
by you?

I painted it as your problem
treated you as broken
and held myself aloft
as healer and whole one
while you subsumed
yourself in grayness

how could I not see that
my subtle shaming
and unconscious blaming
drove you further
underground?

but what was I to do
without you?
how was I to mend
our shattered story
all by myself?
how could I
claim my pain
without causing you
to collapse inward
even more?

I tried to generate
heat and light
through sheer
force of will
but black holes
can extinguish
everything
if you let them

who kindled first?
who passed a flicker
to light the other's wick?

no matter

what's important
is that one of us did
then by that small light
you could glimpse
your beauty
I could sense
my solidity
and we could
begin to see
each other
clearly enough
to bring the bellows
to our love
and thaw our chaffed souls
around the growing flames

you
who I thought
abandoned me
I am sorry
I abandoned you back

you
who I thought
snuffed your love
I am sorry
I let mine gutter too

we
who came back to life
let us celebrate
our resurrection

and accept that
no apologies
are necessary
now

Plate Tectonics

we knew we were enveloped
by shared destiny
we knew it could be
no other way
than entwined for eternity
but that certainty
set us up for a fall

paradise was lived
for longer than was reasonable
until *wham*
a stubborn womb
shook things up

then *crack*
the first child came
and a thin fault line
of separation formed
as I turned my
gaze to the infant
at my breast

then *bam*
another child came
and my focus
went entirely AWOL
as the plates shifted
with a radical jolt

then *smack*
you went missing too
into a gloom-filled chasm
opened by the quake

and *wail*
destiny stumbled
as paradise crumbled
leaving jagged fissures
and sundered souls

and *howl*
we were both lost
without the certainty
of that assumed inviolable bond

then *creak*
I looked up
from my children
and bedrock moved again

then *groan*
you looked up from your misery
and plate rubbed hard against plate

then *thwak*
we collided again somehow
laughing at our clumsiness
and sputtering
welcome back

now
the heaving earth
has settled
the aftershocks
have subsided

and lulled into
new normalcy
we are free
to create a fresh destiny
until the next tectonic shift
jolts us akimbo again

If/Then

if I had not met you
when the sun shone from behind
illuminating your halo of hair
if I had not been flush
with the ecstasy of chartreuse spring
if I had not believed
in magic and true love
as inviolable laws of nature
I would not have had the courage
to utter the word soul-mate

if you had not known the names
of every flower and tree
like nature's gentle interpreter
if you had not felt like home
and smelled like heaven
if you had not promised the freedom
to invent life from scratch
and lit up my dreamscape at night
I would not have wrested myself
from the love of another
to weave a future with you

if we had not talked of commitment
customized to fit a new era
if we had not married legally
knowing the true consecration
had occurred long ago
if we had not settled into graduate school
developing mastery of our fields
we would not have turned our gaze
forward and outward
to the possibility
of creating new life

if we had not tried for five years
to control the uncontrollable
if we had not been tested
and temporarily bested
in our quest for fertility
if after all that we had not finally
puzzled together enough cells
to generate offspring
we would not have ushered into bodies
the two incandescent souls we did

if they had not been balanced male and female
if he had not been logical and linear
and she emotional and curvilinear
if they had not adored each other
like Calvin and Hobbes
and Dorothy and Toto
we would not be a family
of complementary kindred spirits

and if we had not grown from
one to two
to three to four
from me and you
to we and they
I never would have understood
the hollow place
yearning to be filled
with what should have been

Valentine

you are sky
robin's egg blue
with a light wash
of translucent yellow
warming
my upturned face

you are steel guitar
played with a slide
body etched with filigree
voice a resonant twang
moving me
with your melody

you are victory garden
cushioned with mulch
brimming with
berries, apples
tomatoes, peaches
nourishing me
with your gifts

you are rock
folded, molded
in slow motion
showing me
how to live
unafraid of
vast time

Thermodynamics
of a Long Marriage

I'm looking for controlled burn
not wild fire run amok
I'm not asking to be consumed
like I used to

I'm looking for subtle sparks
that can grow
through eye contact
orange embers
that can be animated
by curious questions
flickering flames
that can be fanned by
shifting from
sibling ease
to man/woman desire

I want to burn again
but in a new way

I'm not asking for conflagration
just feeling a bit of
scorch and scald
I want to be safely on fire
using our bodies as kindling
like we used to
only more tempered

the temperature
has fallen
as it will in winter
and we must find heat
where we can

the best I can do
is strike a match
and trust
the warmth
will spread

Tagline

you were prophesied
in my girlhood dreaming
I constructed you
from wisps of fairytales
and tendrils of fantasies

I caught glimpses of you in glades
and shadows of you in the dusk
I saw flashes of your eyes
in the watercolor sky

I expected the rush of flush
when we found each other at last
and I was right
I knew, we knew
when you turned around and
smiled right into my marrow

so I bought the plot
believing *happily ever after*
was our rightful tagline
but I read the synopsis wrong

love is a verb not a static noun
and a love story requires
a tithe of daily choice
especially after
gilt edges curl back
to reveal ordinary paper
and too-perfect calligraphy
ages to more quotidian script

now after thirty five years
of living the tale, I know
our tagline actually reads:
*vulnerably, earnestly
faithfully, fearfully
open-heartedly
ever after*

amen

Earth

Bridging the Gap

on one end I tether
my hammock to a tree

the trunk is an anchor
the roots are tough tendrils
keeping me
earthbound and grounded

on the other end I tether
my hammock to a kite

the windy blue air
holds it aloft
swaying me gently
as the diamond
swoops and soars

my hammock swings
between two realms
because I need both to survive

my body is earth coalesced into flesh
but my spirit expands into light

I honor earthworms, pebbles, and clay
but I long for transcendent sky

I eat from the verdant planet
but I inhale the breath of the breeze

so I tether my hammock
to corporeal roots
and ethereal currents both
swinging, floating, resting
in one strong net
woven between two worlds

We Breathe Together

human is to plant
as plant is to all life
fundamentally the same
in carbon consciousness

we lean toward the sun
we grope for nourishment
we breath together
through nostrils and stomata

vein is to phloem
as artery is to xylem
and I am filled with flow
as are you
green brethren

you are the collective
lungs of the world
and I the individual
with lungs gasping for air

we both feel heat
we both wither from drought
without you I can't survive
but without us
you could thrive

marrow is to heartwood
as vertebrae is to cellulose
you teach me to reach
sky-driven in growth
you show me to bend
when met with
inexorable force

you feed me
inspire me
and in the end
you eat me

I am honored
to fertilize you
become you
ashes to dust
nutrient to nutrient

we root
we bloom
we fruit
animal to vegetable
life force to life force

the delicacy of the dance
of your leaves
and our hands
of your buds
and our hearts
is a mystery
of endurance
in us both

we co-evolve
we quickly dissolve
we sprout anew
from the grace
of soil and womb

bark is to skin
as seed is to hope
and leaf in hand
we move forward
into whatever
changed earth
awaits us all

Speaking Up

I speak for the voiceless
those that slither silently
through black soil
those that writhe and whip
microscopically in pond water
those that crawl and haul
carapaces over pine duff
those that skulk under ledges
in mountain streams
those that offer rubbery umbrellas
as their fungal fruit

I speak for walking sticks
on hair legs with twig bodies
for moths camouflaged
as desiccated leaves
for wasps who lay their eggs
in others' abdomens
for locusts that drive people mad
for cicadas that don't

I speak for rock tripe and slime mold
for liverwort and club moss
for horse's tail and foam flower
for jack-in-the-pulpit and columbine

I speak for lichen like burned paper and
lichen fizzed as chartreuse beard snarls and
orange lichen bellying up the rock face

I speak for chameleon and pangolin
for bat eared fox and honey badger
for lesser bilby and long-fingered aye-aye

I speak for lilac breasted roller, reticulated giraffe
red-legged frog, maribu stork
and slow-witted, peaceable manatee

I speak for sea pork and nudibranch
for river otter and bat ray
for shrimp and oyster

I speak for basking shark, minke whale
sea turtle, white pelican
and weird-eyed, one-sided halibut

I speak for leopard shark and leopard seal
and just plain old leopard

I speak for douglas fir and jeffery pine
for dogwood, redwood and sequoia
I speak for live oak and quaking aspen
for maple, elm and chestnut

I speak for those who walk, crawl, swim and fly
and those who sprout from soil
all cry through my voice
asking me to form words
for those lacking lips and tongues
and vocal cords to vibrate out their misery

the voiceless ones
use me to translate
bleat and scream and whistle
squawk and growl and howl
into words
so that we may hear
their collective message
focused down to
one pinprick
point
one clear
simple
plea:

STOP

so we might live

Existential Crisis

an ant carried inside
clinging to a crimson leaf
scurries to escape
back into her colony

she bustles with urgent purpose
then finally halts in lonely futility
an individual separated
from her formicary
a cell severed
from the communal body
wondering about oneness
alone and with others

the ant would give her life
for her comrades
sensing if the group survives
her genes live on
but dying alone
is a death without meaning
a loss without purpose
for the organism she serves

I lift the red leaf
and the ant rides it
into open air
still searching
for collective wholeness
to soothe her solitude

I release the leaf into a pile
of curling, crinkling brethren
and the ant zigzags away
into the autumnal flames
where she can
live out her duty
or sacrifice her spark
for the slow burn
of the common good

Bristle Cone Pine

grizzled elder
clinging to granitic soil
for countless centuries
sipping bare nourishment
from the stony earth
your panoramic view
scopes back to time before time

you have perfected survival
minimally exerting life force
to produce spartan needles
only as needed

you stoically withstand
unrelenting wind that curves your spine
pelting rain that twists your arms
blowing snow that blizzards around you

inexorably you grow
cell by slow cell
while far below
we whiplash through puny lives
flailing with self-importance
rushing with frenzied blood

your sacred trunk testifies
to the wisdom of patience
your branches beseech us
to reach for the yellow eye of god
your roots teach us
to practice steady search and grateful suck
wherever sustenance is found

bristle cone pine
let us protect you
to save ourselves
let us know you
to open ourselves to grace
let us feel your slow life
shimmering like mercury
in our veins

Acorn Wisdom

I am acorn
swollen and split
polished and pointed
prickly chapeau cocked at an angle

I know how hard it is to be born
how much energy is needed to catalyze growth
how much ornery drive it takes to
expose tender greenness to uncaring elements

I know how easy it would be to surrender
and fold back into withered stillness
yet how fiercely
life fights to be expressed

I know how to read the faces of the moon
the moods of the sun
and the idiosyncrasies of water
seeping, dripping, flooding, trickling

I know how to turn tender stem
into rough bark and stalwart trunk
I know how to caress the sky
with fingers of leaves

I know how to shelter opinionated jays
support acrobatic squirrels
and repel deer teeth
with sharp leaves of leather

all this lives inside my meat
my cracked belly exposes my embryo
but my wisdom is protected
and curled inward as inviolable potential

I wait to become oaken
to unfurl into fullness
over summers like dry tinder
and winters punctuated by Vs of geese

I am ready to grow
into what I know

Redwood

your aroma wakes me
like a slap from a Zen master
it slices with clean clarity
from the slender leaves
growing at your tender tips

during life
you stand as a silent sentry
stolid and sure in the slowness of time
when you die
your emptied husk
nourishes the forest floor
and your love sprouts offspring
in a circle around your ghost

you are a good mother
and your steadfastness comforts me
I am compelled to bury my nose
in the clefts of your bark
and wrap my arms around you
in filial embrace

your wisdom is root-deep and sky-high
your discernment grows
as you witness creatures
living lives of frantic industry
at your feet

redwood
show me
how to slow my metabolism
so I too can feel the seasons

show me
how to accept earth sustenance
so I too can have faith
in the long-term good

show me
how to awaken
with the sharp scent of sagacity
so I too
can become a sentinel of stability
in the face of
relentless time

Wind Breaks

cypress trees grow in upsweeps
sculpted by wild winds
green hair blowing inland
stiffened by salt spray

elemental forces
gnarl them, twist them, train them
into streamlined shapes
with sideways leans

they relinquish the vertical
slanting diagonal
with the will of the wind
the incessant wind
the victorious, ubiquitous wind
that gales off the ocean
skimming salt from wave tops
and sand from beaches
corroding and blasting
whatever tries to retain form
gusting, howling, blowing
with lungs of infinite stamina
wearing away resistance
with fierce inevitability

until the wind stops for a breath
and in the rare moment of rest
the cypress creak their relief
crack their limbs
straighten a bit
to see if they still can
then hunker down for
the next inexorable blast

I pull my windbreaker tight
around fragile skin
envying the thickness of bark

Cumulus Sky

red-tail hawk perches
silent and keen
scanning to fuel its flight
but nothing stirs

striated wings spread
updrafts lift
bird spirals heavenward
then looks down

there
emerald grass shivers
there
gray pelt streaks across meadow

now
raptor folds wings tight
plummets like a bullet
aimed with precision

scurrying vole
senses shadow
dives for hole
a micro-moment late

scaly toes
with stiletto talons
close around
pulsing life

earthbound vole
becomes airborne
in fright and flight
before entering the void

hawk gulps sustenance
borrowing blood from another
then flies with reconfigured vole
into the cumulus sky

Dragonfly

cellophane wings
scribbled with hair-thin veins
plum-twig body
shellacked with black
compound eyes
multiplying facets of flora
in holographic pixels

reed walker
water swooper
prey seeker
mosquito zapper
zigzagger
deft and fierce
as a fighter pilot

rider of wind
buddy of box turtle
living jewel
immortalized with
ink strokes
on rice paper
by a hand
long gone
to bone

haiku incarnate
spirit of lake
brethren of heron
winged observer of
carp and koi
biological biplane
mirrored in
rippled, stippled water

dragonfly
weighing nothing
tamed by nothing
fragile as breath
free as air

Life From Another Planet

life from another planet
is as close
and as far as the sea

tiny animated iotas
undulate membranes
and filter feed with feathers

monstrosities
open black-hole mouths
and suck in whole universes

scaly creatures
fluoresce in a dance
and seduce entranced prey

transparent jellies
pulse like flowery hearts
and sting with poison daggers

sleek submarine forms
cruise with menace
and gorge in crimson frenzy

tube worms
wear lipstick
and kiss around scalding vents

coral coordinate
the many into one
and synchronize hide and seek

we, too, are strange ones
born of
the amniotic ocean

our blood surges with tides
and droplets of salt tears
fall like sea specks on our cheeks

Gifts of the Pacific

brown pelicans
splintering water
into prismatic droplets
and rising with bulging gullets

flounders flatly
skimming the sandy bottom
eyes swiveling
strangely on one side

cormorants drying
salt-soaked wings
as though crucified
by the sun-warmed wind

surf scoters whistling
as they flap into flight over
loons bobbing
in formal attire

gray whales rolling
to expose barnacles
and spy with one eye on
land-locked beachcombers

orange and purple sea stars
shining in the depths
and clinging to craggy rocks
with palpating tube feet

kelp swaying their
mucilaginous fronds
and supporting primeval forests
on tiny flotation bladders

succulent green anemones
gaily waving pink tentacles
then closing to a puckered goodbye
when the tide inevitably goes out

Chef's Special at the Darwin Cafe

the recipe:
create a teeming, steaming
molecular broth
spice with lightning
bring to a roiling boil
on the geothermal stove

simmer slowly –
let coacervates cool and
coalesce into cells
that clump and divide
in fast-forward evolution
turning soup into stew

stir well –
let cell clusters grow
sprout nervous systems
gills, tails, fins
until creatures drag themselves
on bony elbows
out of the warm bath

keep stirring –
as they pop legs, tails, wings
to skitter, slither, soar
as they squawk, bleat, shriek
grunt, tweet, roar
to proclaim
I Am Here
forevermore

keep stirring –
until a beast sits upright
stands tall, stretches legs
to stride, lope, sprint
to dance nimbly
for the sheer joy of it

stir in a new direction –
let brains burgeon
with wrinkled wisdom
and craniums kindle
with awareness of self and other

stir some more –
as each flame flashes
for a millisecond
before giving way
to whoever's turn is next
and the fireworks of life
ignite and extinguish
in the bright night

scrape the bottom –
notice fecundity flourishing to excess
in one invasive species
procreation running amok
hungry mouths gorging greedily

skim scum off the surface –
as more sparks animate more flesh
like a house of mirrors
reflecting infinity
some are struck down
some fall down
but more arise
too much survival
of the fittest
renders them unfit
to survive

dump the dregs –
shout from the back
dinner is done
kitchen is closed

carefully clean up
the vast mess
put away pots, pans, lids
ladles, knives, whisks
lovingly shove
the last customer
out the door saying
that's all there is
there is
no more

Shells and Bones

slimy-fleshed mollusk
you were no more or less
than tissue and shell
a complement of hard and soft
not so different from me

you created a spiral home
tender as the ear of a newborn
curling into satin intimacy
of shadowy chambers
where sea ghosts whisper still

you fortified it
with spines and spires
erecting crenulated ramparts
of calcium carbonate
to protect your vulnerable core

your masterpiece
has outlived you
and speaks to me of
strength and fragility
curved into one seamless whole

I carry my shell on the inside
nothing to see, everything to sense
will it outlast my supple skin
to speak to others
as your shell now speaks to me?

if my body lived elsewhere
my bones could jangle
on a shaman's necklace
or dance percussively
on the ankle of my enemy

my skull could evoke reverie
on an altar to nature's cycles
or weather beneath the desert sun
to the gray color
of your muscular flesh

but my hardness will most likely
disintegrate into mulch
in the forgiving soil
delighting blind burrowing ones
not unlike yourself
or incinerate
in a crematorium
flaming and flaring
with wild abandon before
collapsing in a heap of velvet ash

mollusk
my skeleton answers your shell
sensing a comrade in mortality
ours is a conversation
of softness and hardness
evanescing into
water
earth
air

Home Address

am I my body?
do I peer out from within the twists of DNA
dance inside caverns of mitochondria
and sip the yellow yolk of each nuclei?

or am I my mind
the designated driver of this animate machinery
the wizard behind the curtain who knows more
than the animal in which she resides?

or am I my heart
seat of emotional hurricanes
and halcyon days housed
in a bloody mechanical pump?

or could I be my soul
that ineffable wisp of essence
that fickle animator ready to bail out
when the physical going gets tough?

where am I housed?
where do I crouch clinging
to my illusory but irrefutable
me-ness?

and what is left
when my body withers to dust
my mind-hum dims to silence
my heart becomes still
and my soul flies free?

Tangerine

plump, pregnant fruit
your juicy vitality
is cradled in elongate cells
your shiny skin
is contoured with pockmarks
your concave umbilicus
is a ghostly attachment
to the mother tree

she bore blossoms
on her fingertips
that fertilized into fruit
now you bear seeds
in your belly that
hold embryonic trees in theirs
your lineage telescopes
toward the hopeful future

tangy offspring of summer heat
when winter wizens you
and rot works its stealthy wonders
you sacrifice yourself
to fertilize your sheltered seeds

your fragrance that beckoned
turns cloying and stale
your juice, once protected elixir
now dribbles and drains
your supple orange dermis
dries to a brittle husk
and in an offering to the earth
you fall and release
the sun and rain
you borrowed

as your brilliance fades
into browns and grays
you liberate your descendants
into well-primed soil
to carry your fruiting forth
with shoots of chartreuse
to adorn the spring

Life Cycle

I remember being a slender stalk
reaching for the sun
feeling my white roots explore the loam
seeking a sure foundation

I remember being a bud
tightly bound by becoming
considering what color I would wear
wondering what beauty I would hold

I remember opening into ripeness
showing off my stamen and style
flirting with silken petals
attracting with sweet nectar

I remember blooming into love and loss
and the innate cycles that sing us home
now I can hear the distant horizon
beginning to hum my song

what happens after flowering?
is there new growth
once petals dull and fall?
can I still create fresh seeds
to carry my colors forth in coming seasons?

I want to blossom until spent
suck life through my vascular system
until my veins collapse
search the soil with my roots
until their tips grow tired

and when the wind comes
I want my indigo petals
to flutter the sky like confetti
celebrating each risk taken
each secret exposed
each love lived

until all that's left
are my silent seeds
sleeping in dark earth
waiting to be called again

Apprentice

how can we
let our bodies sink
into the mud
from whence we came
with a grateful sigh
instead of
desperate struggle?

how can we greet
the comfort of clay
and let go into
the heavy holding
of moist earth
with a sense of
reward after
a job well done?

these sweet
bodies
coiled through
with softness
and strength

these bright
bodies
that let our light
seep out through
pores and eyes

these hurting, healing
bodies
that move us
so well
through our
lightning lives

how can we
part ways graciously
without clinging
or blaming
or demanding
never-ending servitude
from one who has
served so well
or impossible loyalty
from one who by nature
can be faithful
only unto death?

how can we allow
our atoms
to disperse
into ingredients
for new creations
and our essences
to shimmer
like aurora borealis
in an electric sky
without
fearful holding on
to terra cognita?

I don't know

I don't know
but I can glimpse
the desire
for blessed rest
that must creep in
to bones tired of holding
organs tired of toiling
hearts tired of beating
even though still filled
with aching love

how can we let
these precious bodies
sink into the silt
and truly believe
that love and light
endure even while
matter and energy
endlessly change form?

I don't know
I really don't know

but I am an apprentice
trying to ready herself
even now

About the Author

Cynthia Leslie-Bole is a writing coach, editor, and *Amherst Writers and Artists Method* group leader with thirty years' experience helping people explore, expand, and express themselves effectively. Her workshops and one-on-one coaching sessions motivate writers to develop their voice, polish their manuscripts and achieve their publication goals.

Cynthia has led many workshops using creative arts as methods of inquiry and exploration. She has also taught environmental communication courses for UC Berkeley Extension, the University of Delaware, and Executive Enterprises. As a consultant, Cynthia has advised and trained corporate clients in all aspects of communicating effectively with the public and the media.

In addition to her professional pursuits, volunteering to support and develop teen writers gives Cynthia great satisfaction. She judges for the annual middle school Youth Ink contest in Orinda, California, and leads teen writing seminars at the *She's All That* yearly conference in Danville, California. She also provides editorial support to Voiceflame, a nonprofit that takes the AWA method to Malawi, Africa, to promote cross-cultural exchange and the empowerment of women through writing.

Cynthia's writing has been published in the online journal *Rootstalk* and Moonshine Ink's *Creative Brew*. She lives in the San Francisco Bay Area with her best friend/husband and is the mother of two amazing young adults. This is her first full-length collection of poetry.

Acknowledgments

My deepest thanks go to Karen Mireau of Azalea Art Press for her unflagging friendship, creative genius, and generous spirit. Without her, this book would not exist. She is the catalyst behind this collection, and her dedication to collaborative publication knows no bounds. Karen is a literary midwife of the highest order.

Thanks also to Sally Bolger, my beta reader whose keen eye helped me clarify and refine the final draft; to Mary Tuchscherer of Voiceflame International and Laura Wine Paster of Word Garden East for being my writing mentors; to Pat Schneider, the founder of the *Amherst Writers and Artists Method*, for opening the path that I have followed for ten years into the heart of my creative self; and to Mary Oliver, my permanent poet laureate.

And to my fellow writers, with whom I have co-evolved over ten delicious years of playing with words, my heartfelt thanks for sharing the journey with me.

In *How the Light Gets In: Writing as a Spiritual Autobiography*, Pat Schneider says:

> Daring to be seen, daring to let the truth of the human condition be made visible by our telling, whether that be in words or in some other form of witness, splits open the world. Cracks it. And that's how the light gets in.
> (p. 176)

Thank you to my family for supporting me as a writer, loving me as a human being, and helping me find the courage to allow myself to be seen and let the light pour in.

This book of poetry by Cynthia Leslie-Bole
can be ordered directly at www.lulu.com.

Learn more at: www.cynthialesliebole.com.

For interviews with the author,
please contact the publisher at:
Azalea.Art.Press@gmail.com
510.919.6117